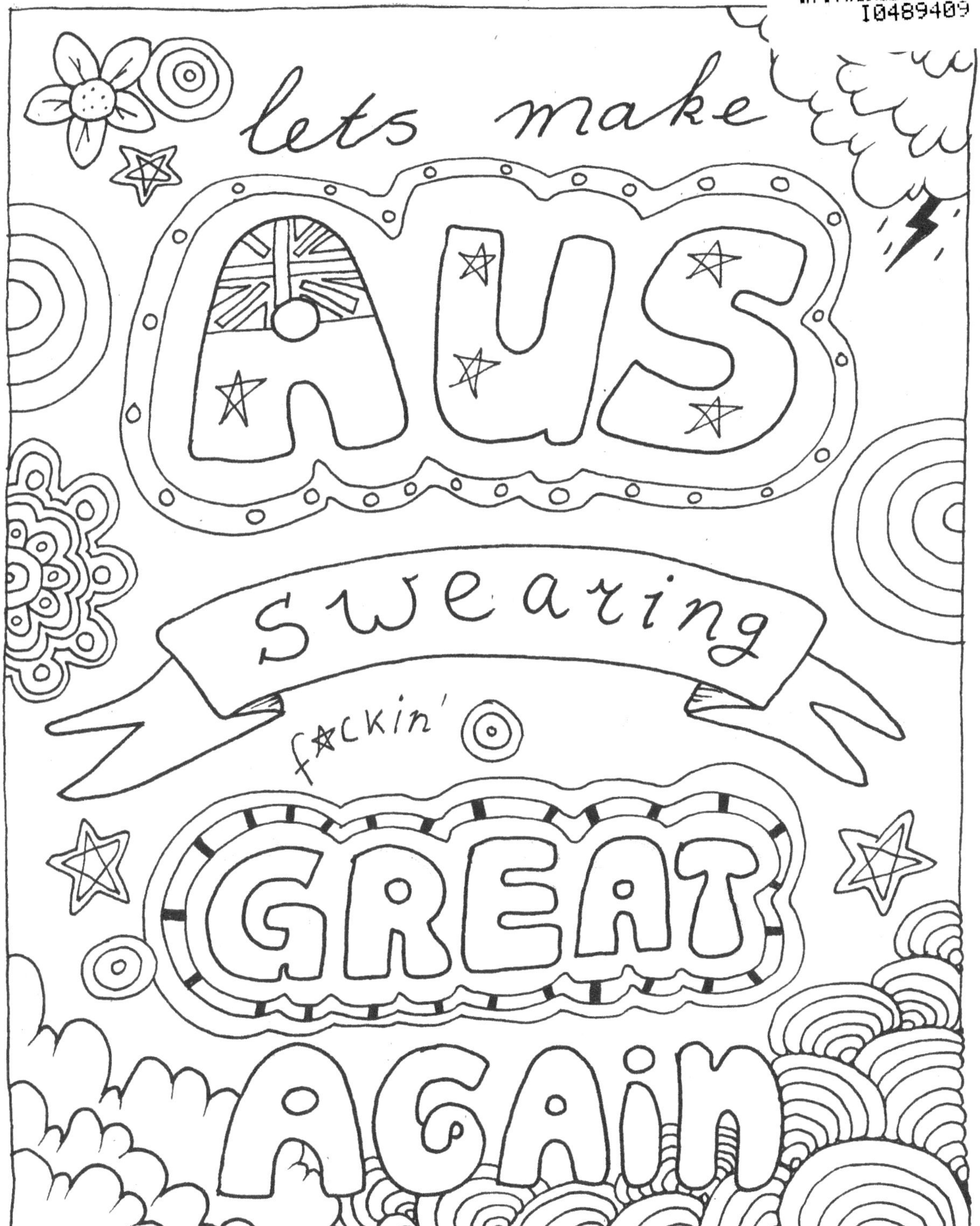

Adult Swear Word Colouring book by MindBodyColor

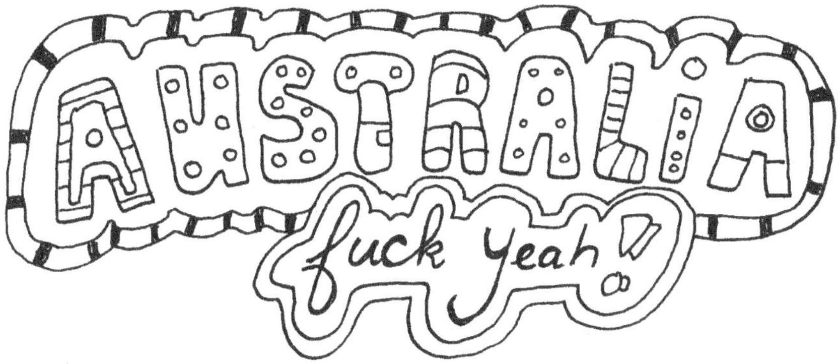

A Swear Word Adult Colouring Book

Make AUS Swearing Great Again.

BY MINDBODYCOLOR

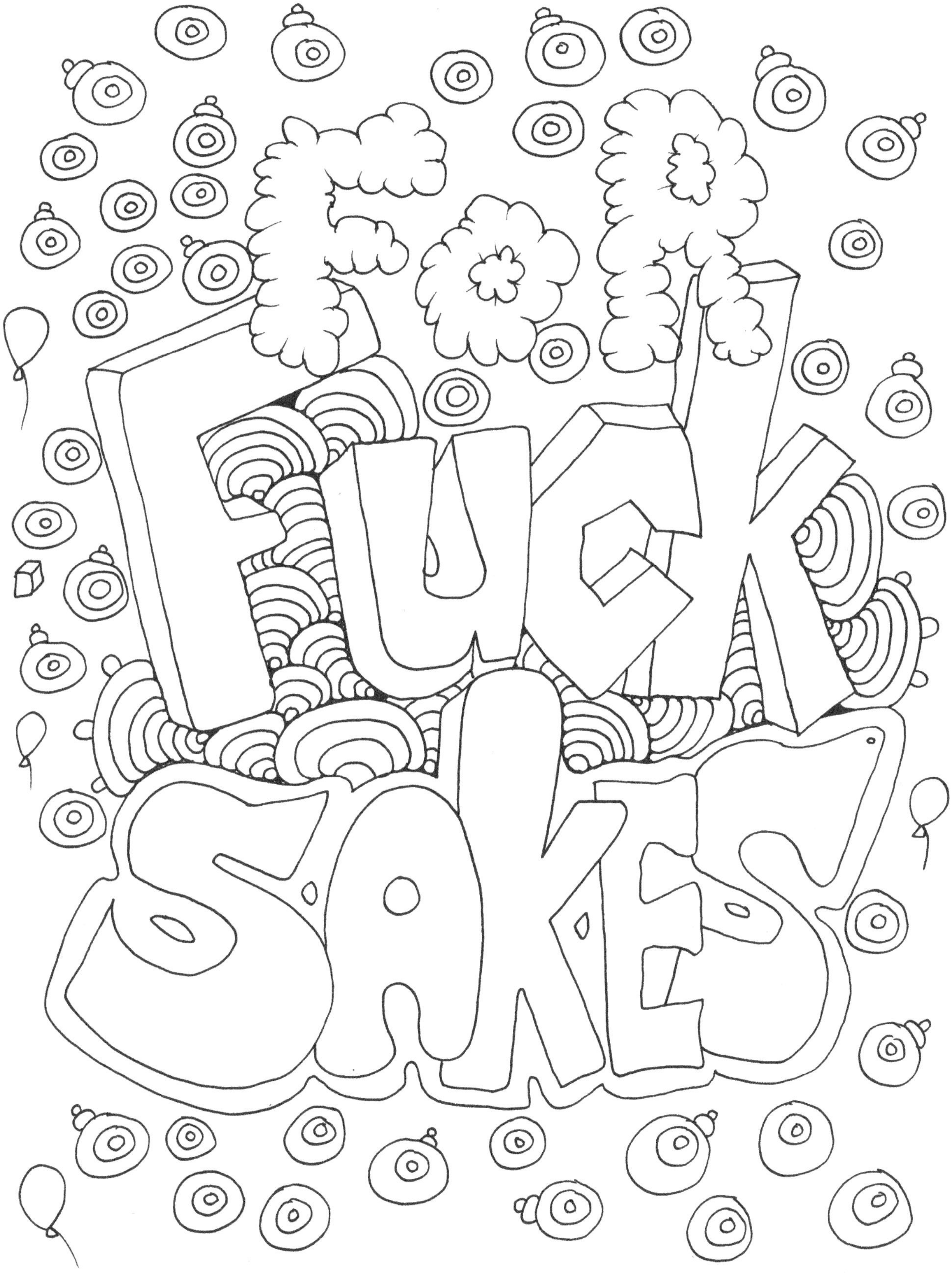
For
Fuck
Sakes

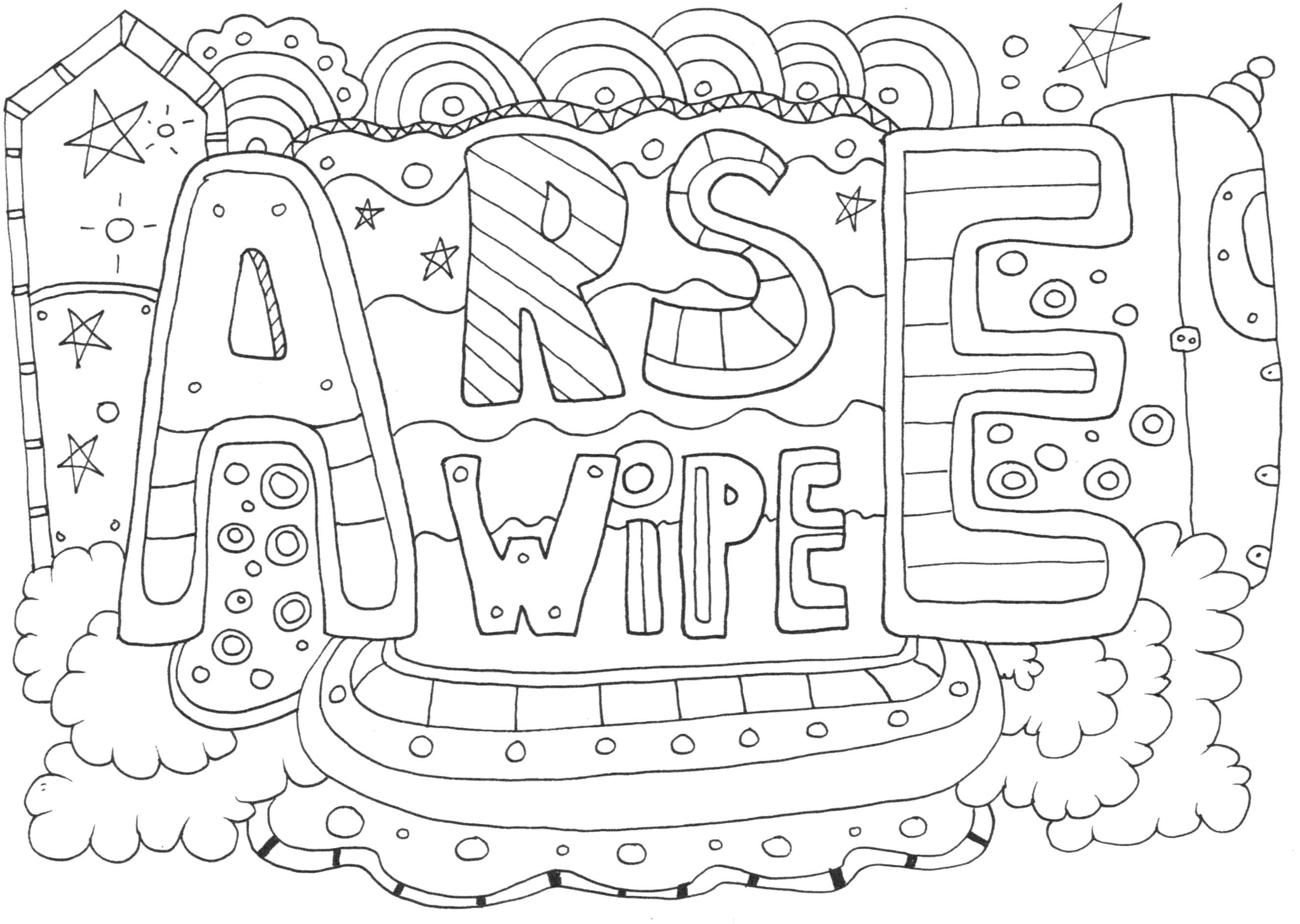
ARSE
WIPE

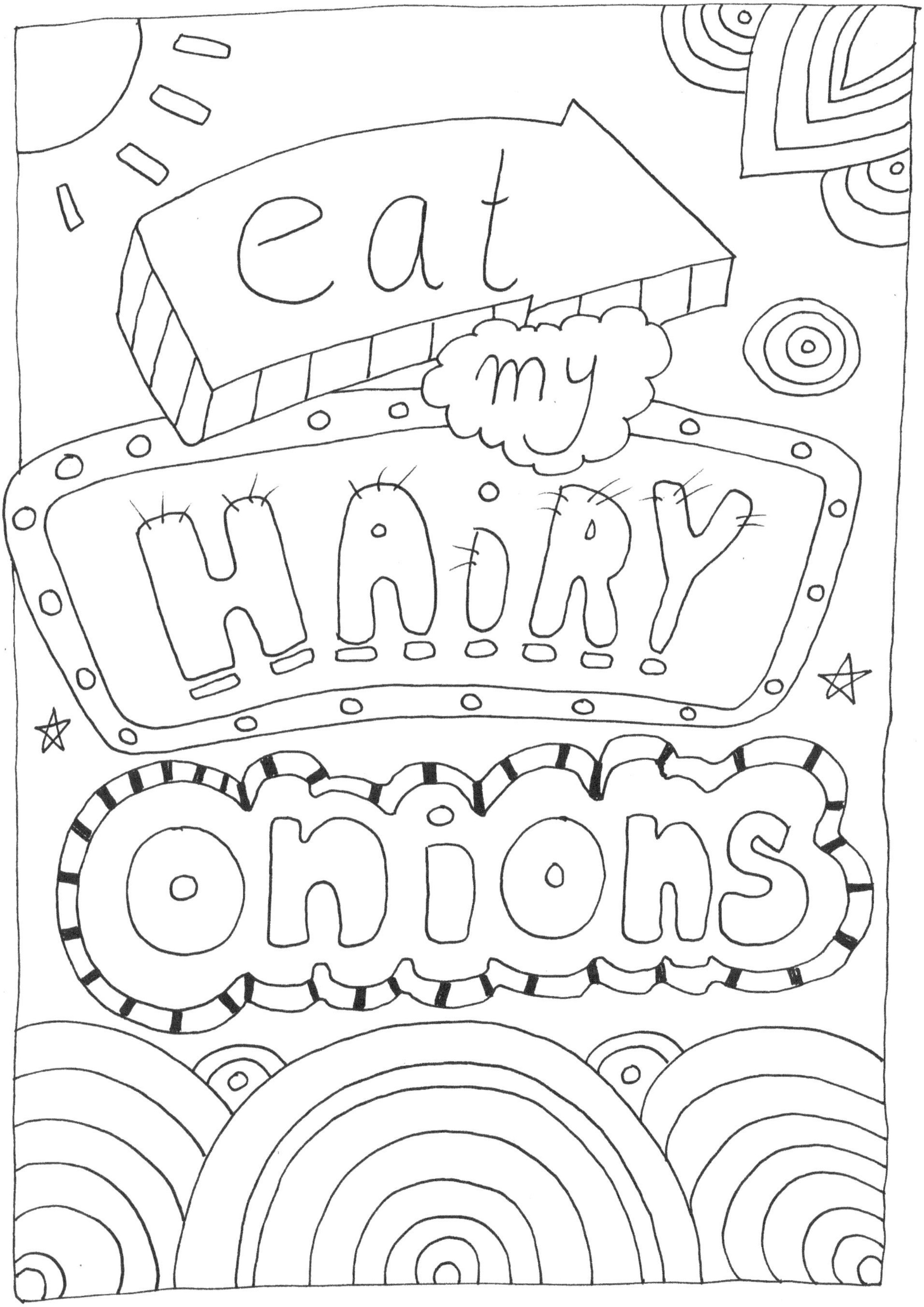
eat
my
HAIRY
onions

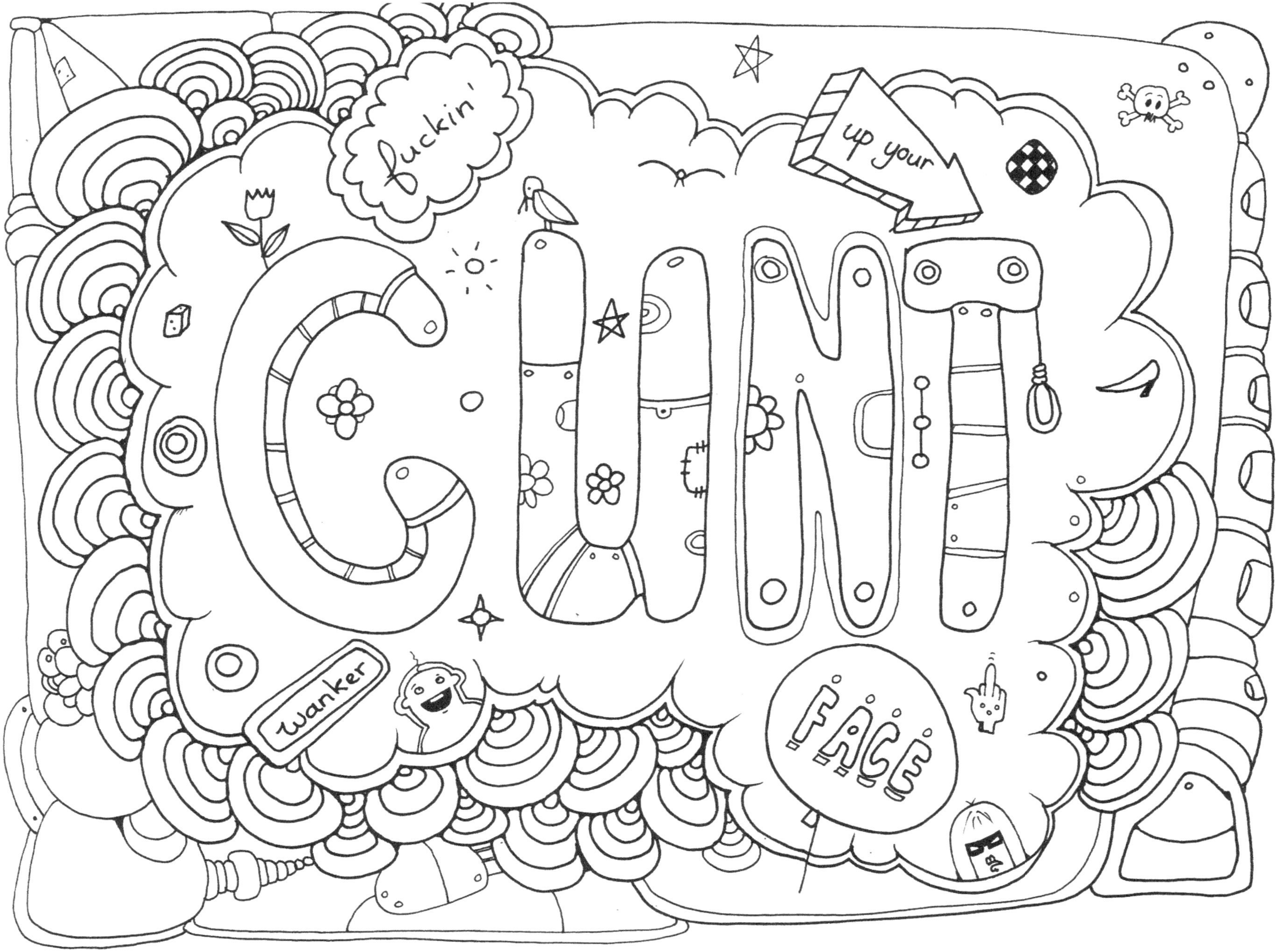
fuckin'
up your
CUNT
wanker
FACE

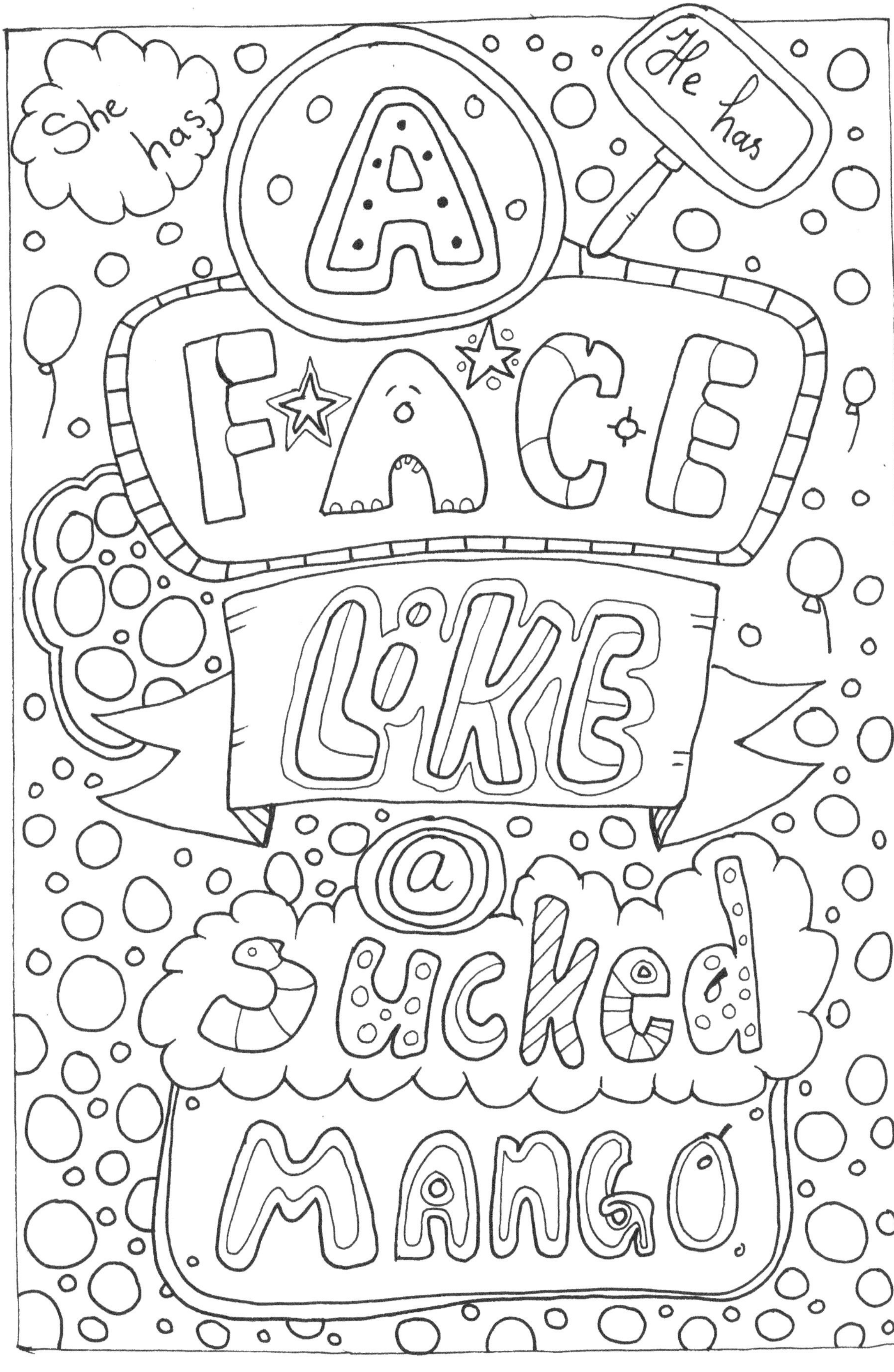
She has
He has
A
FACE
LIKE
@
SUCKED
MANGO

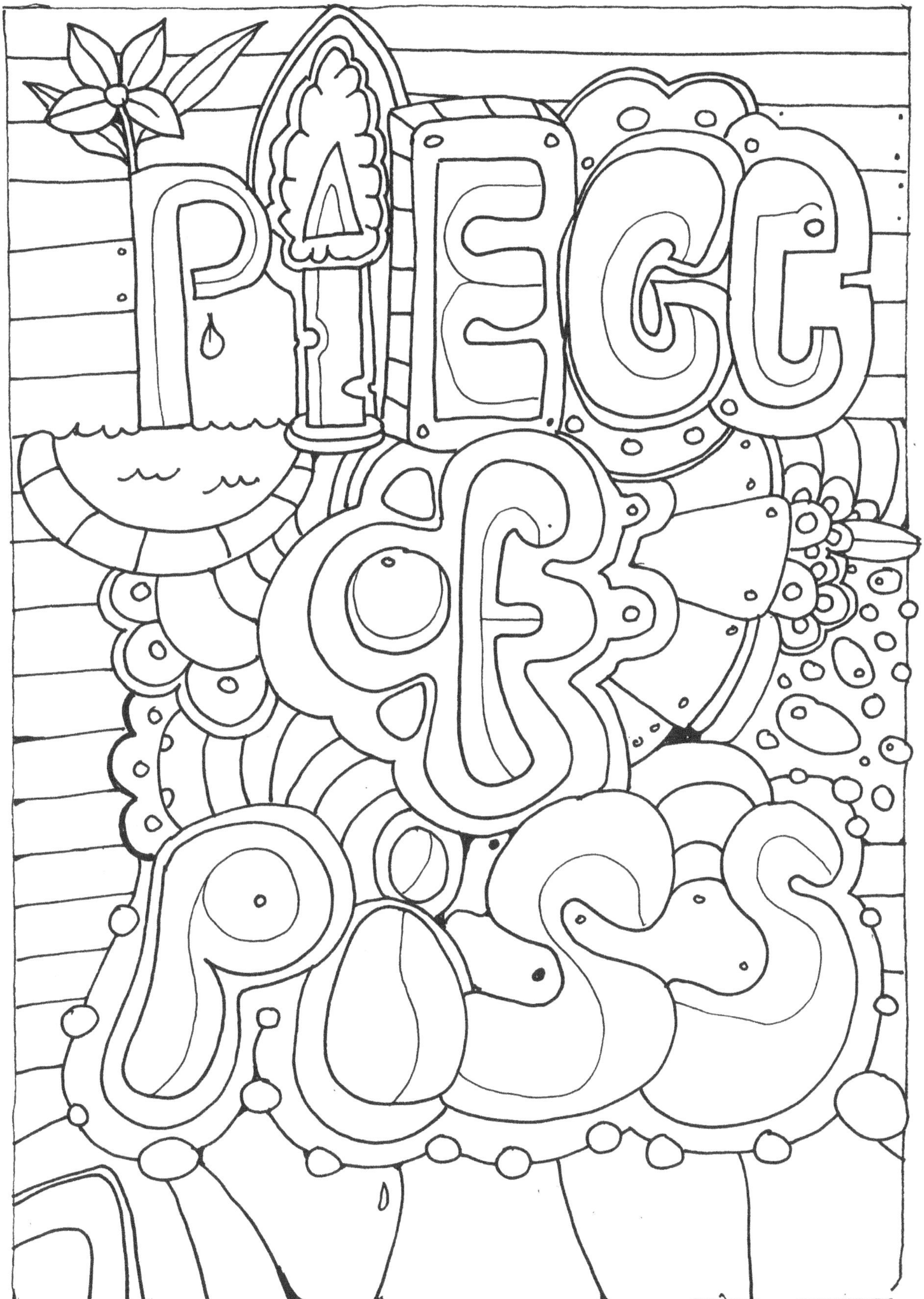
PIECE OF PISS

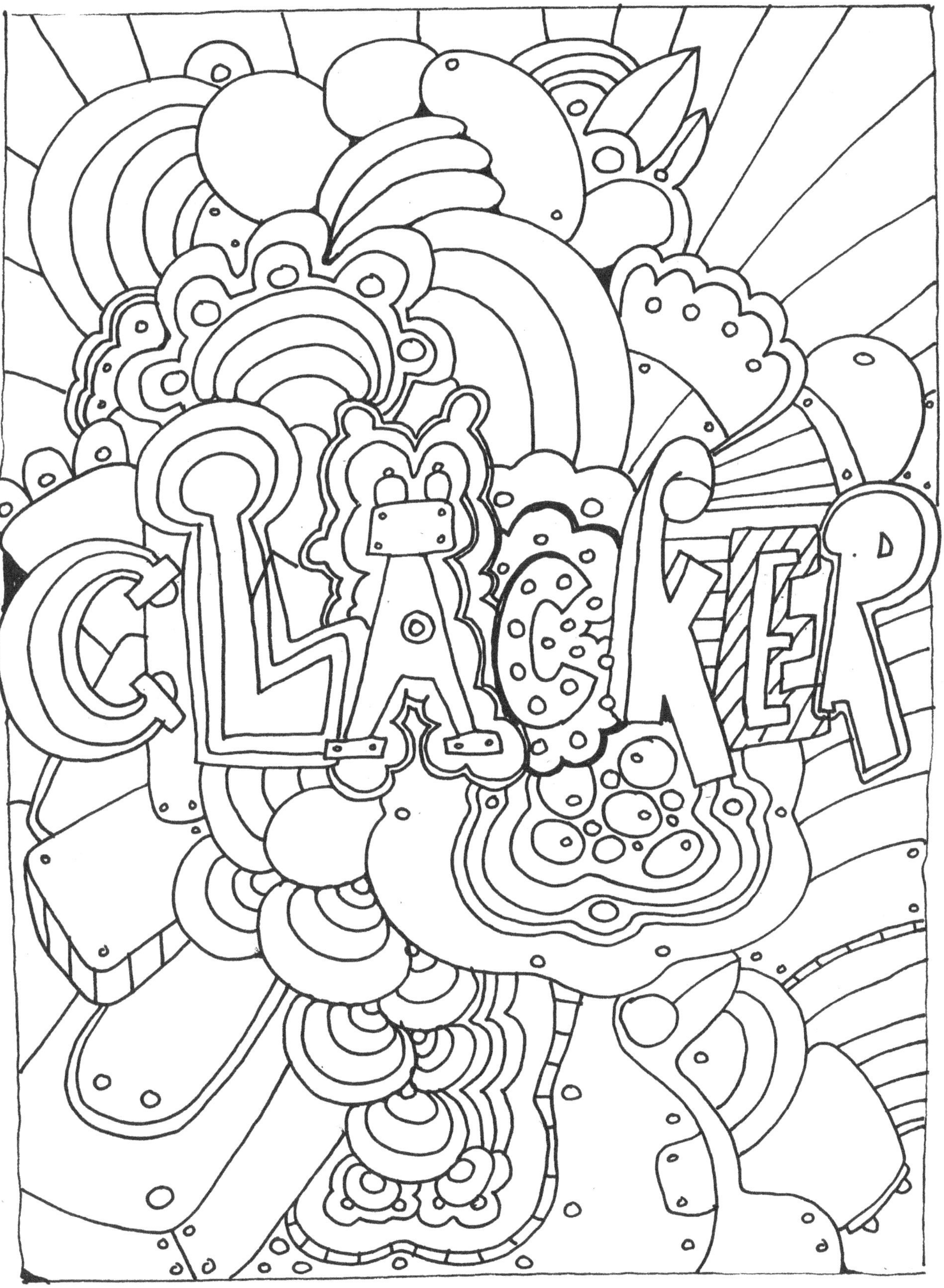
CLACKER

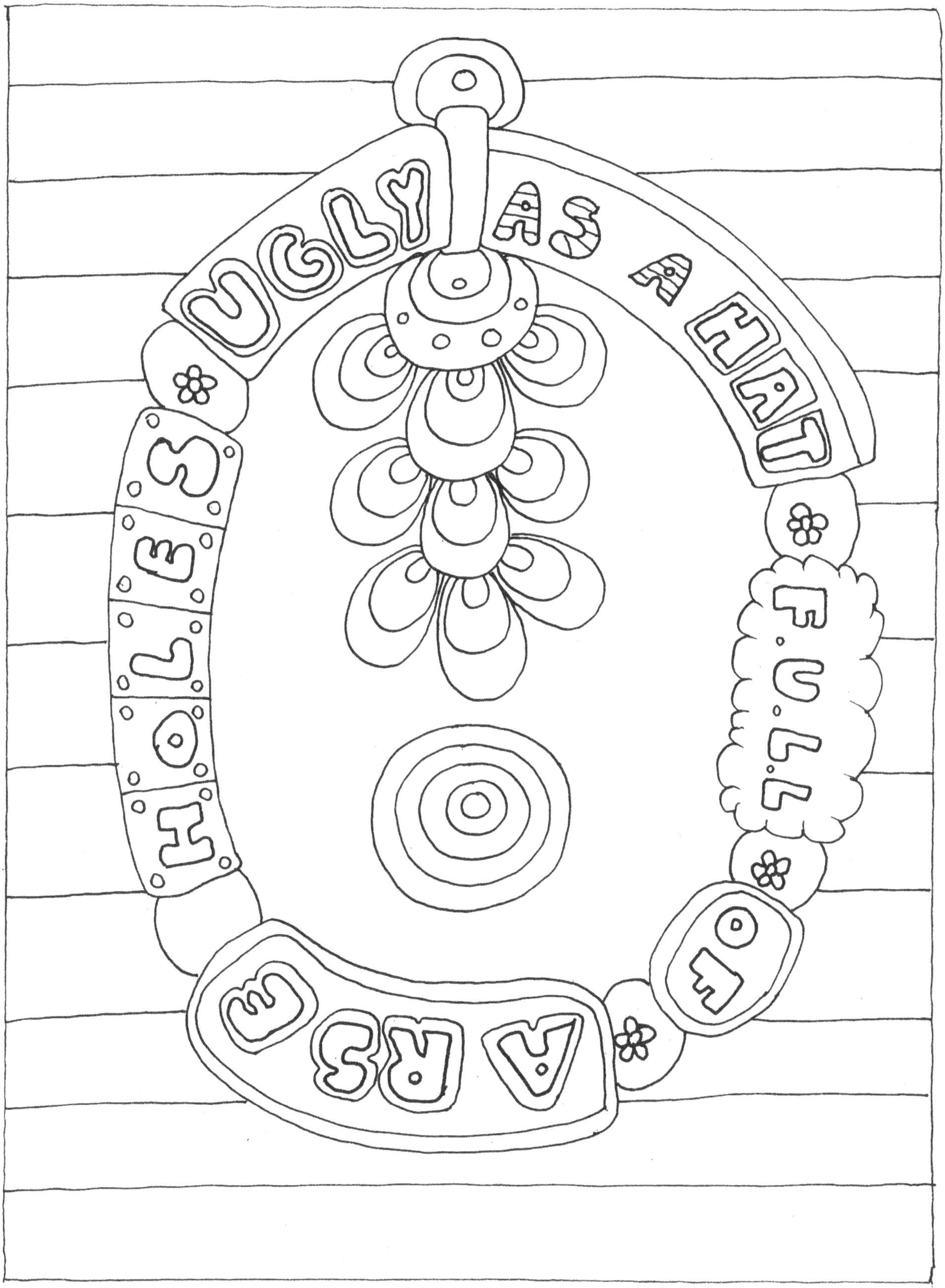
UGLY AS A HAT
FULL
OF
ARSE
HOLES

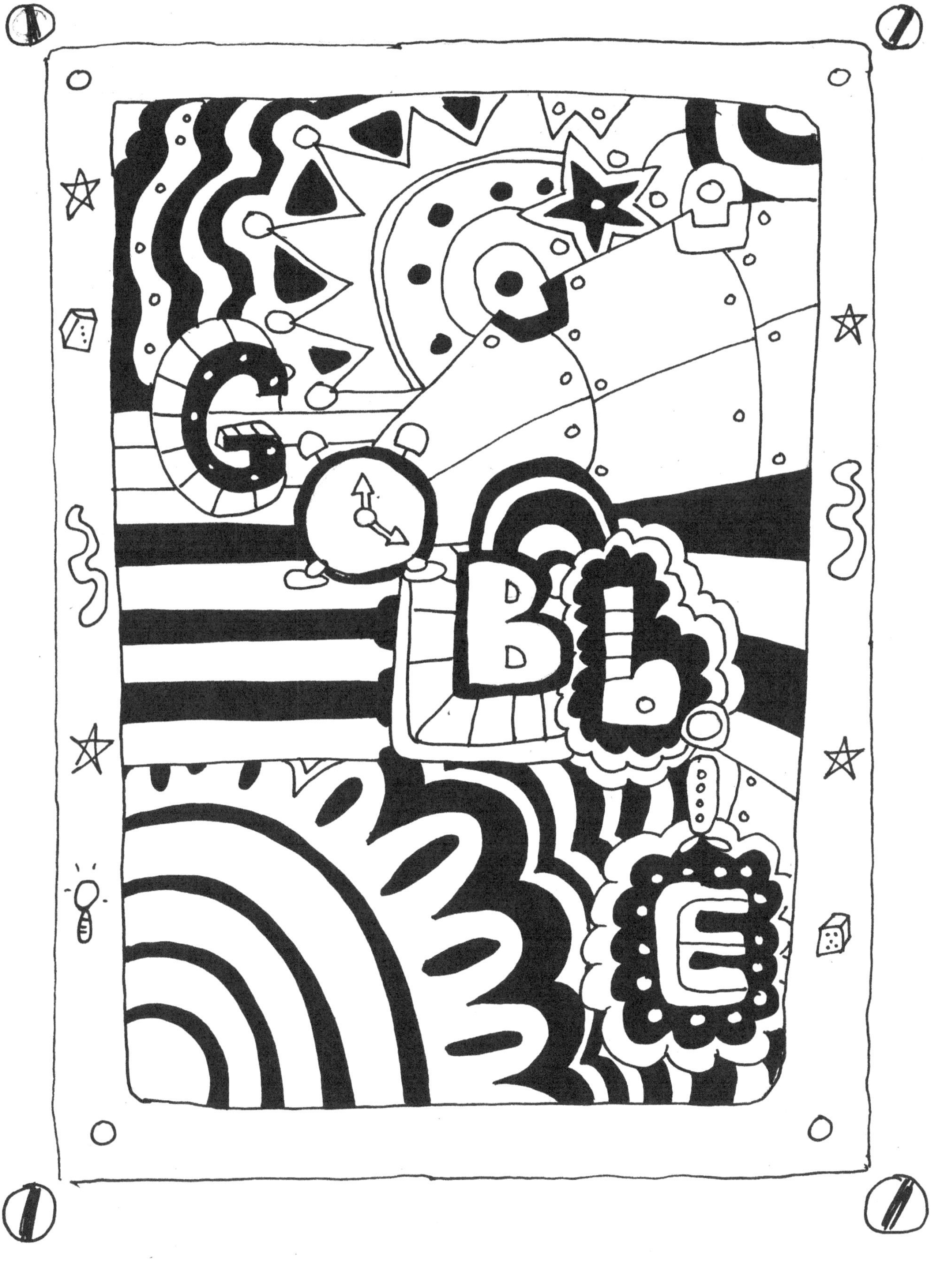

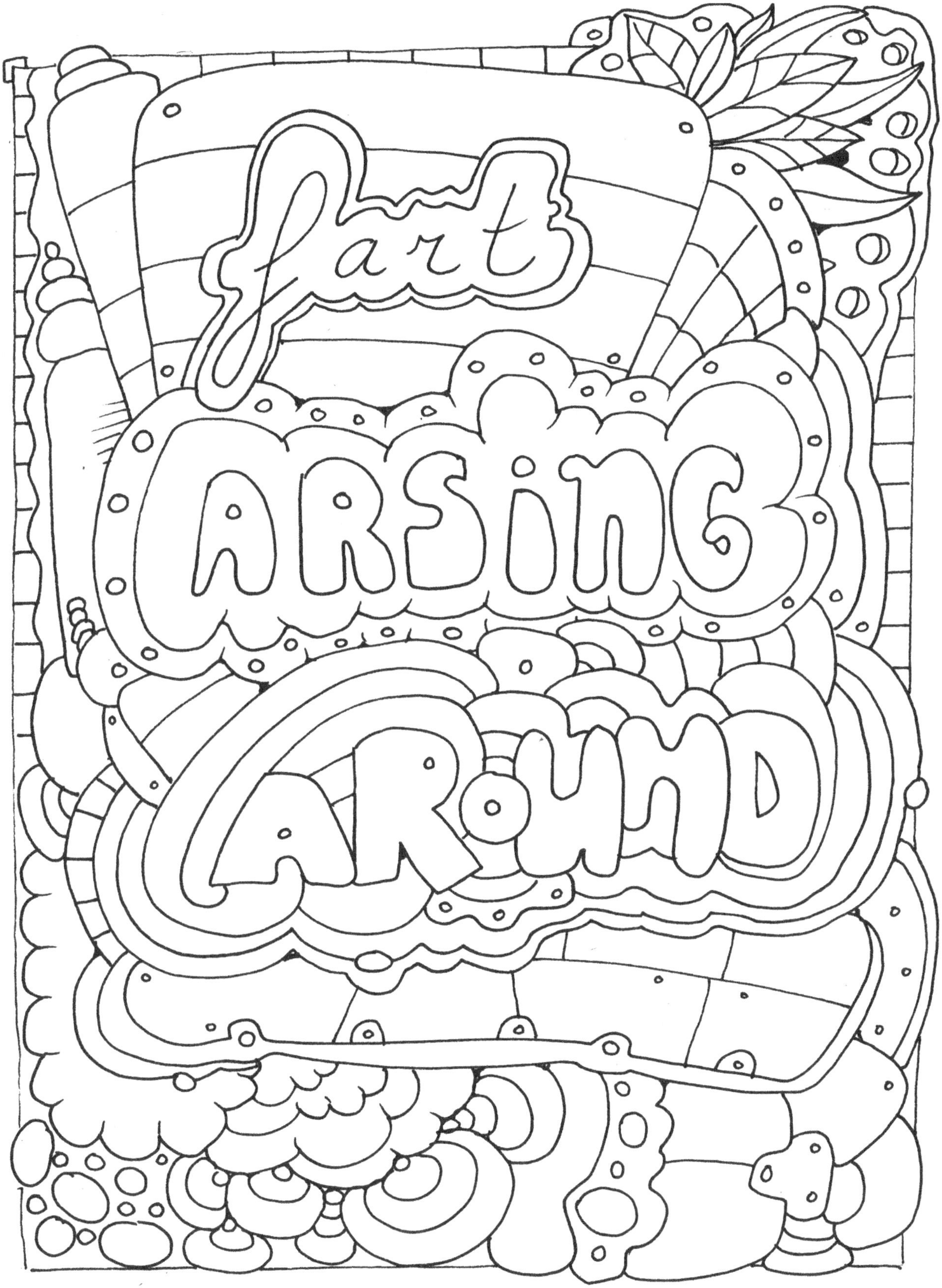
fart
ARSING
AROUND

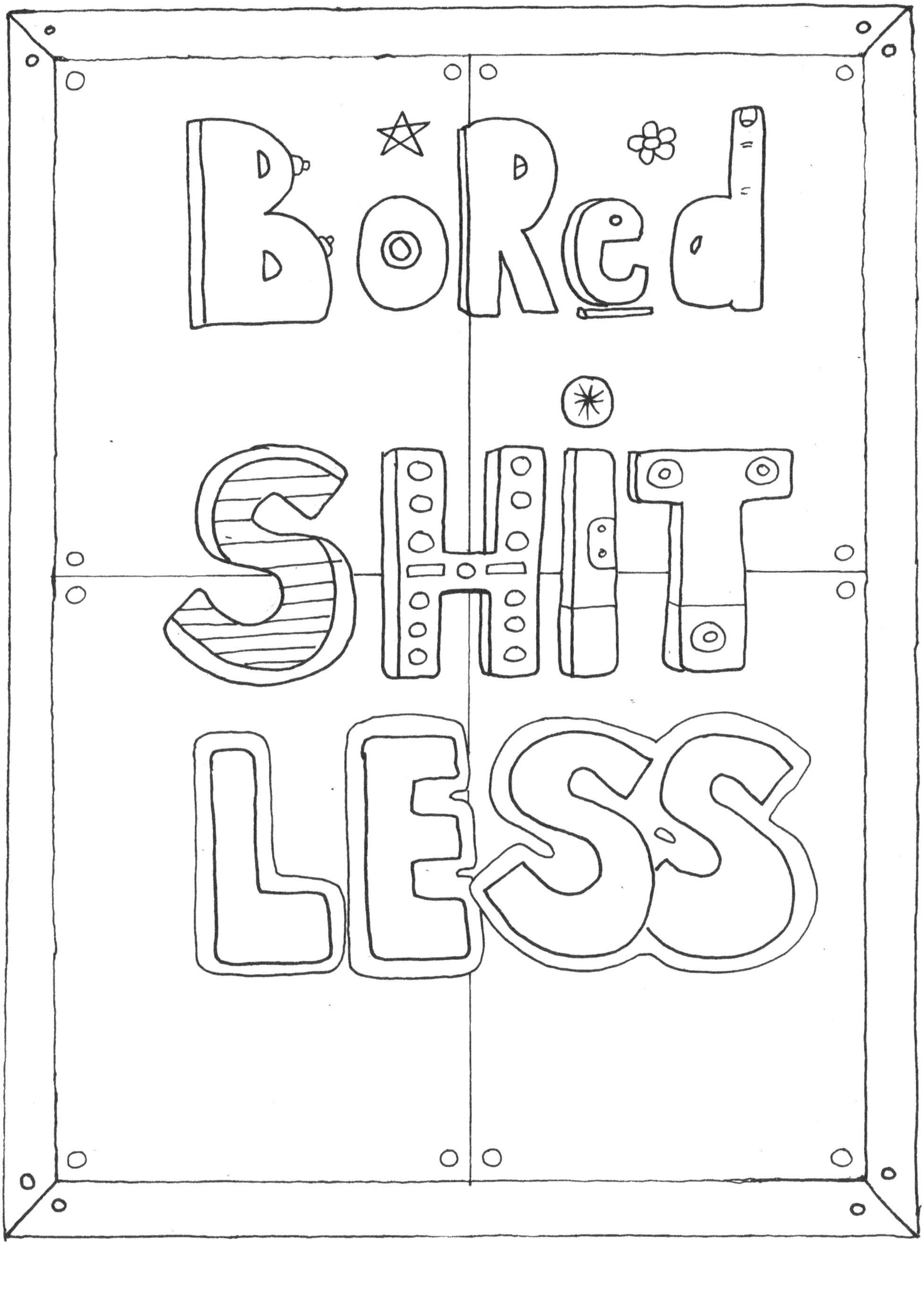
BoRed
SHIT
LESS

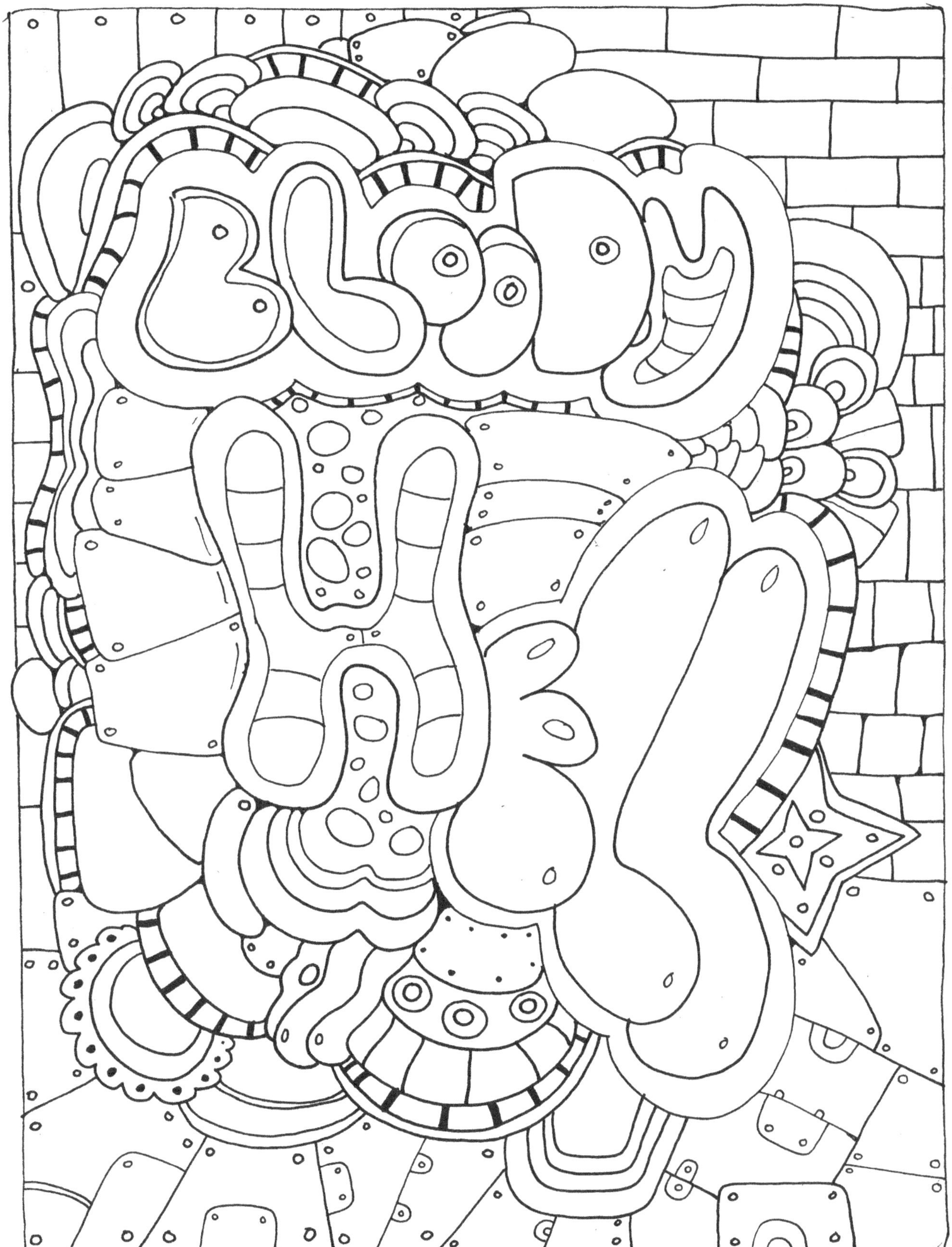
BLOODY
HELL

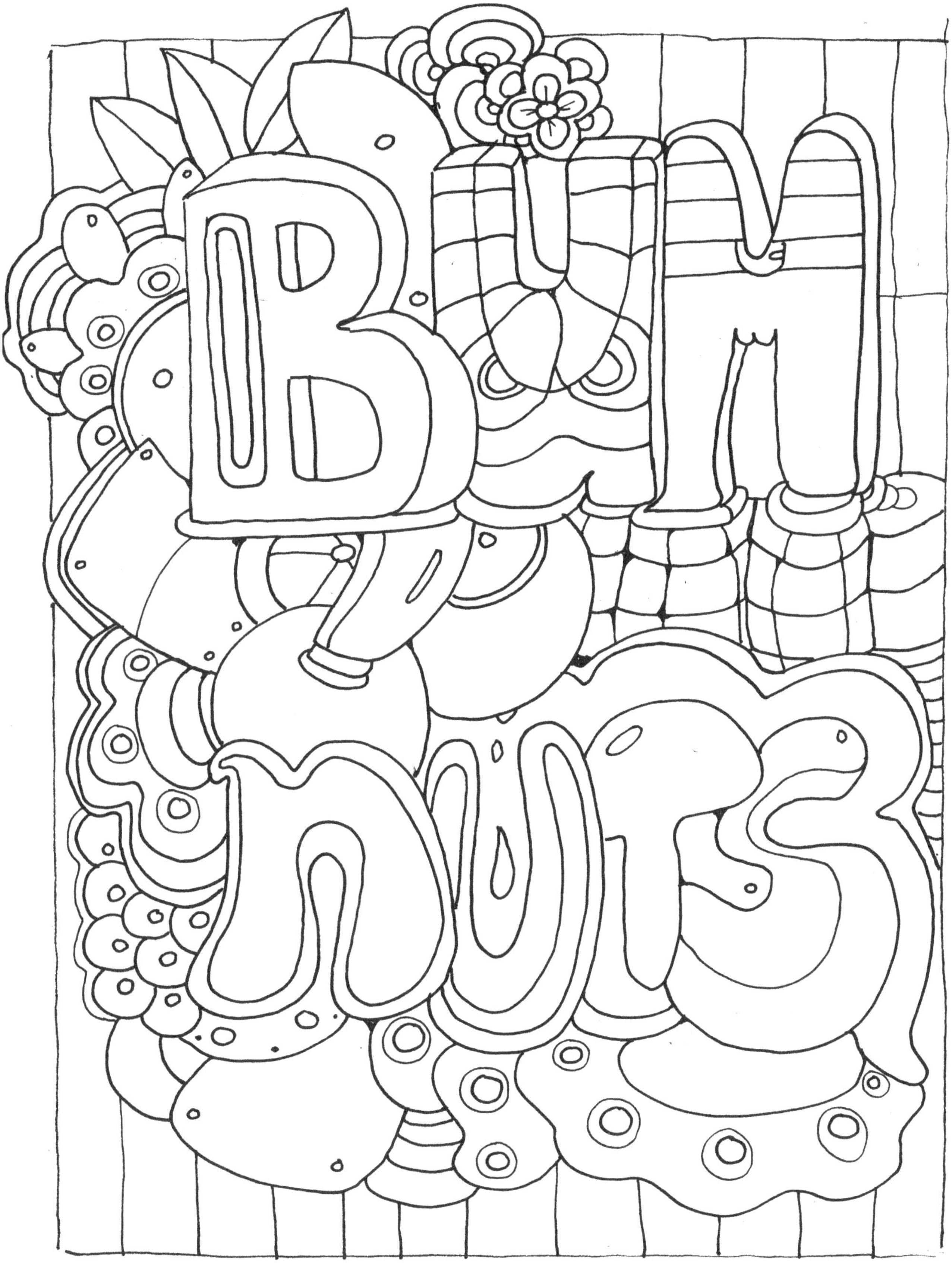
BUM
NUTS

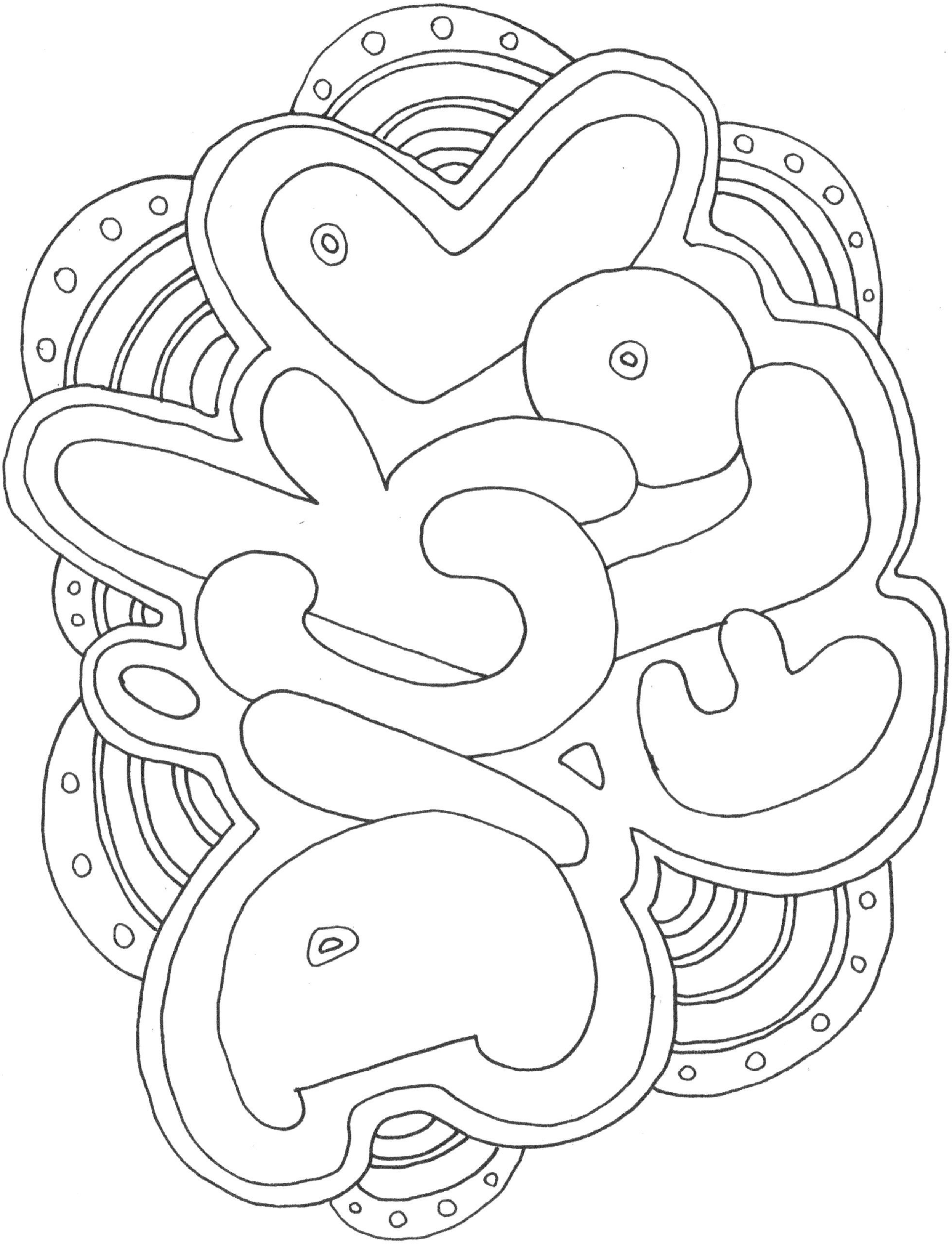

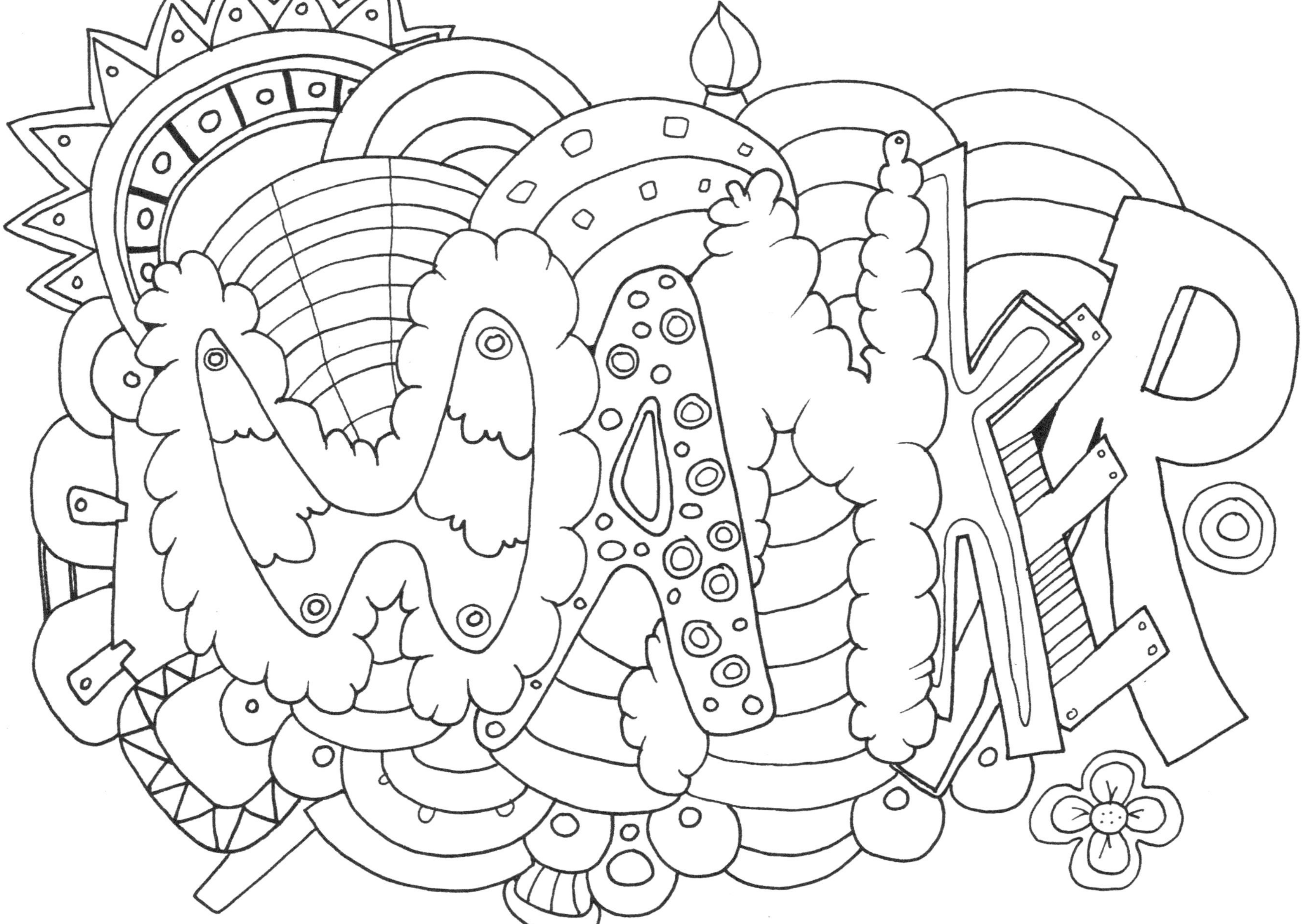
WANKER

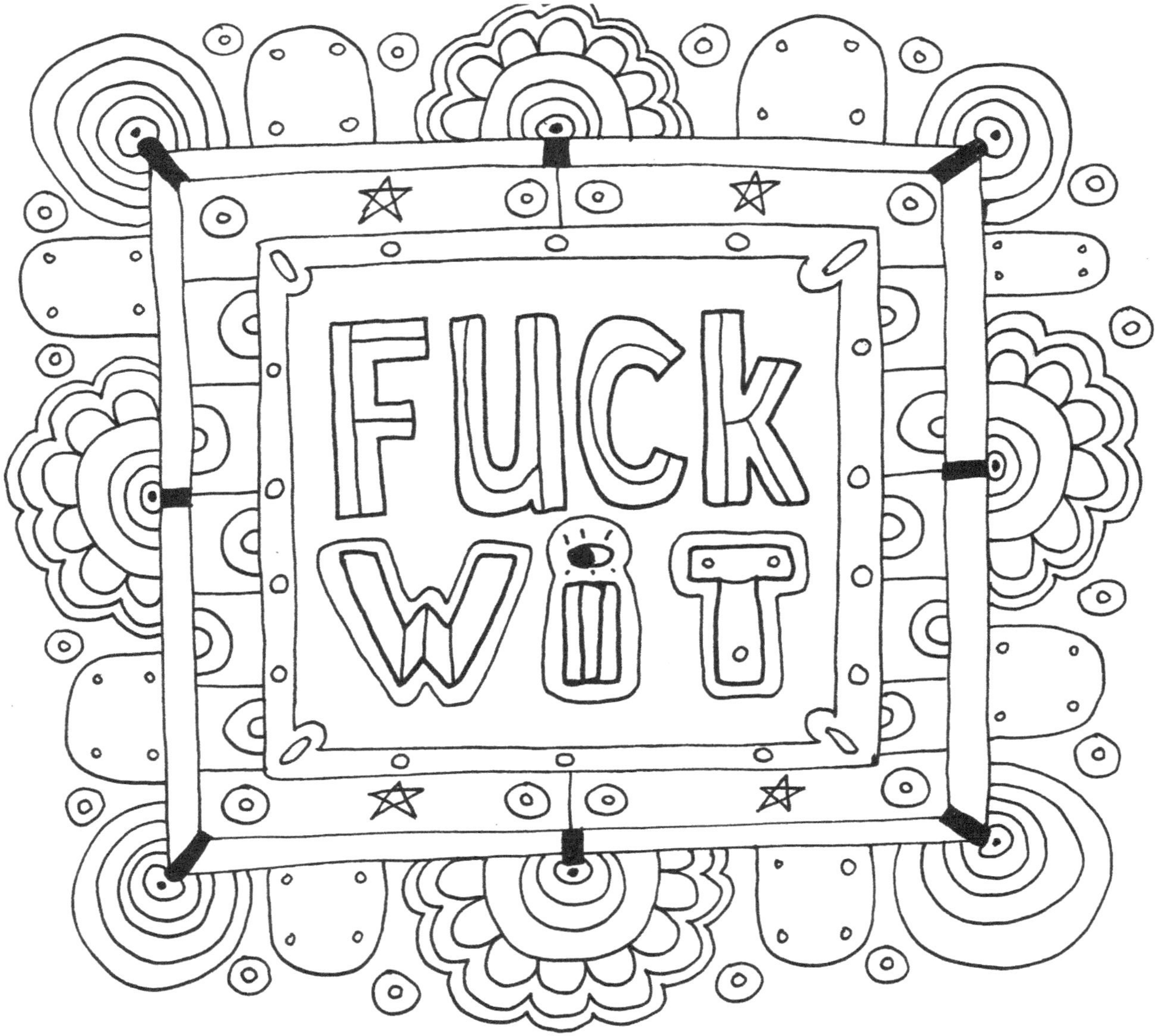
FUCK WIT

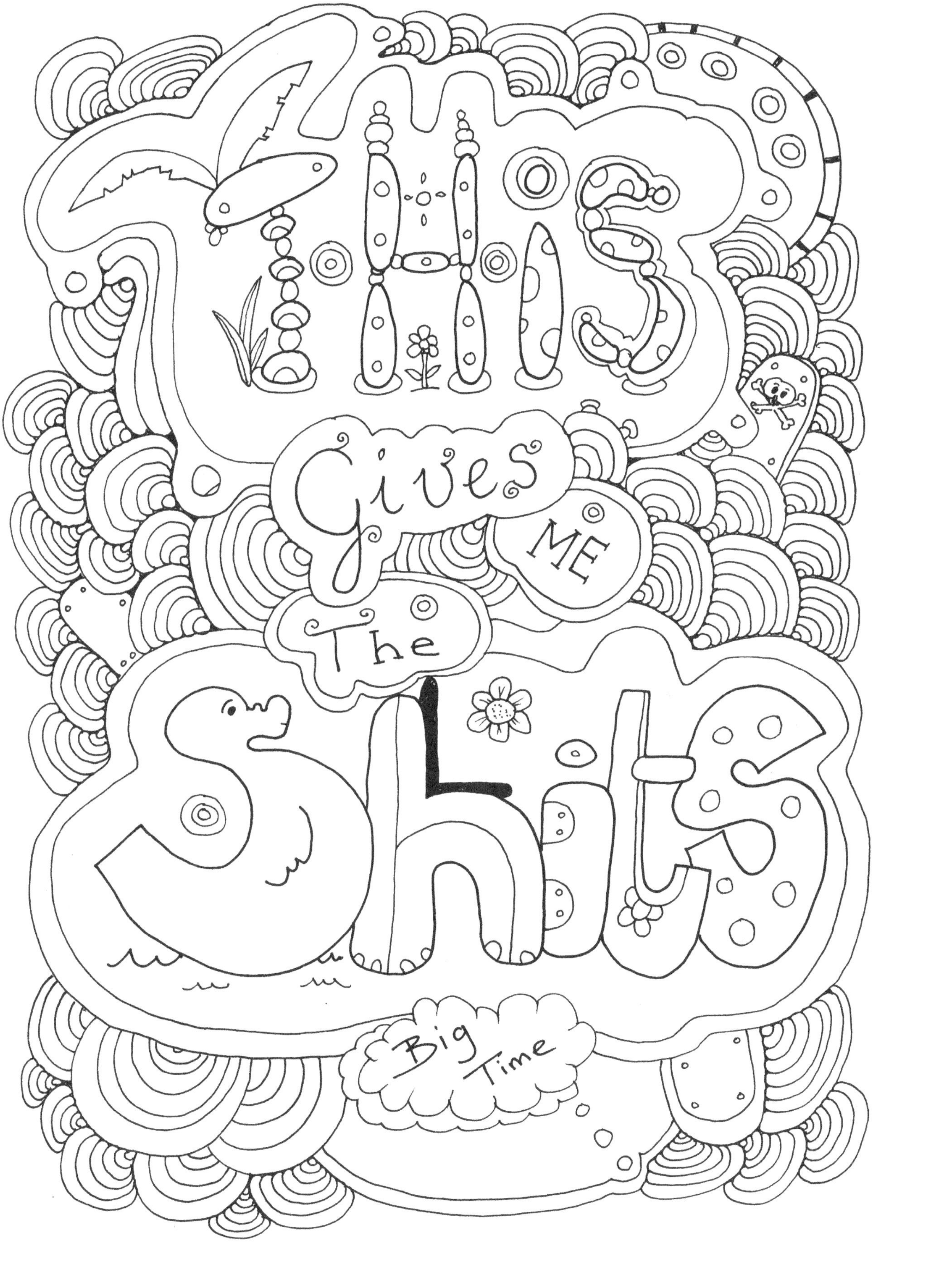

This
gives
ME
The
Shits
Big Time

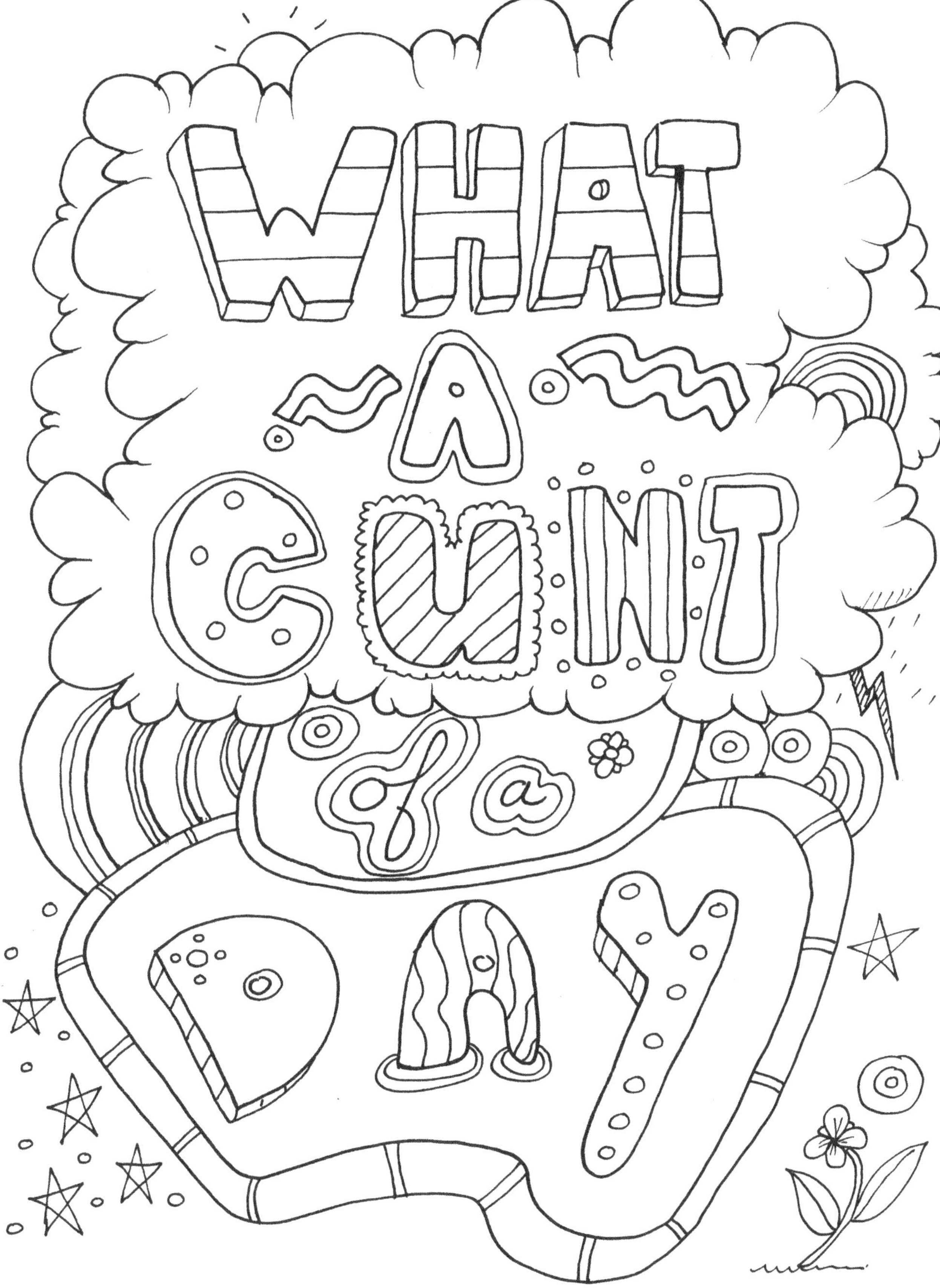
WHAT
A
CUNT
of a
DAY

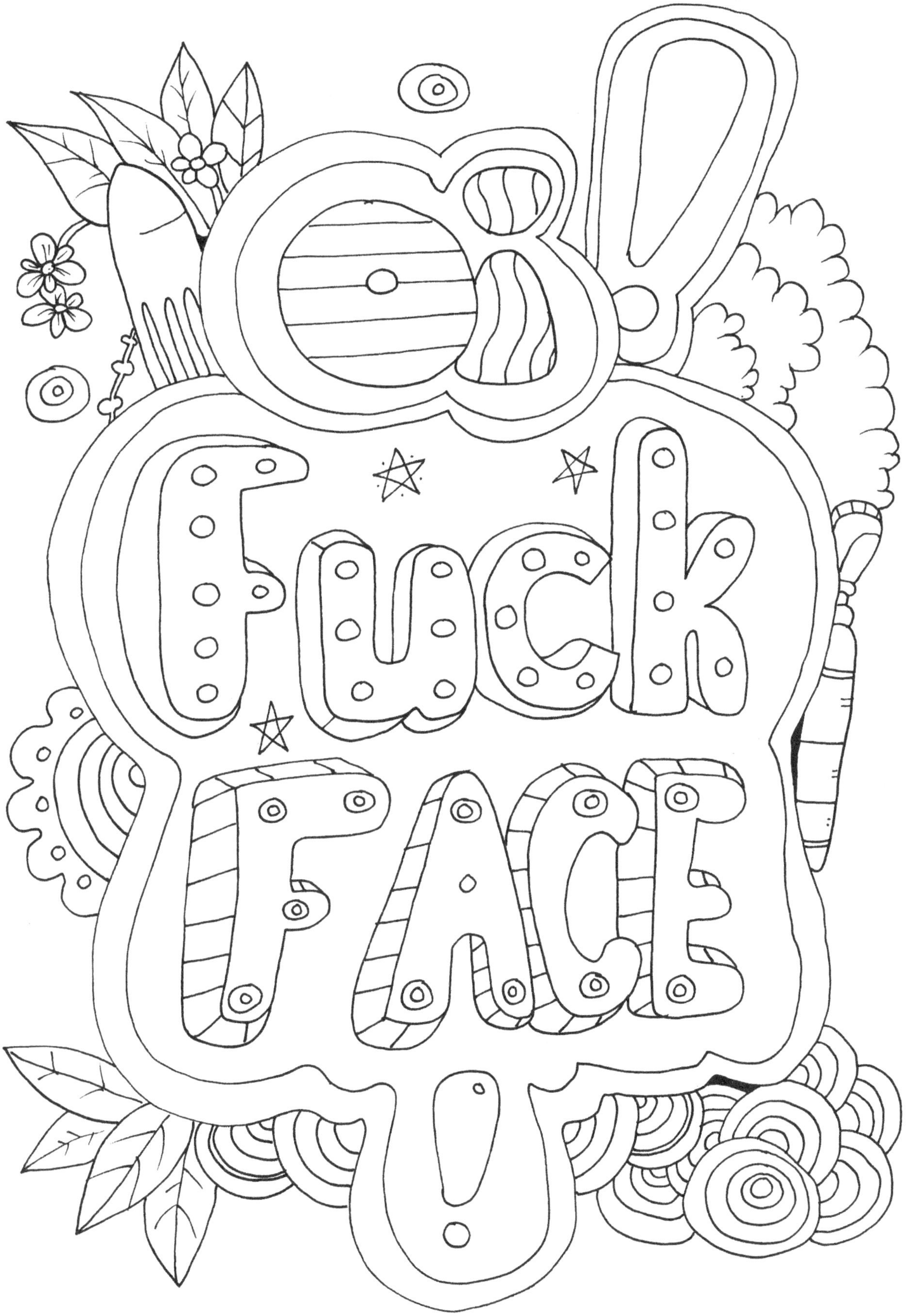
Oi!
Fuck
FACE
!

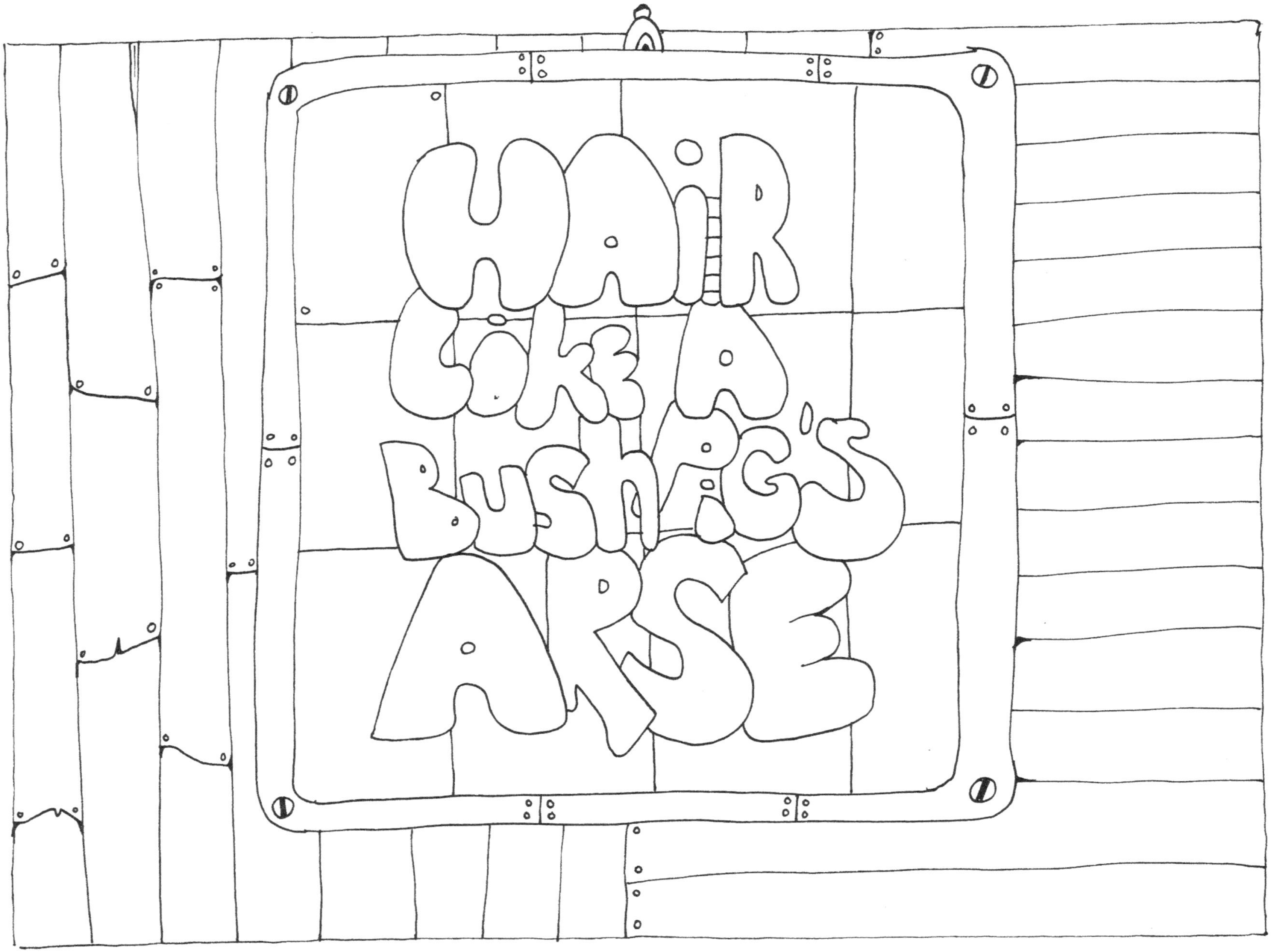
HAIR LIKE A BUSHPIG'S ARSE

www.ingramcontent.com/pod-product-compliance
Lightning Source LLC
Chambersburg PA
CBHW081238170526
45165CB00009B/3095
9781548872809